LITTLE BLUE BOOK
Edited by E. Haldeman-.

Sex and the Garden of Eden Myth
A Collection of Essays on Christianity
Maynard Shipley

Martino Fine Books
Eastford, CT
2024

Martino Fine Books
P.O. Box 913,
Eastford, CT 06242 USA

ISBN 978-1-68422-940-6

Copyright 2024

Martino Fine Books

All rights reserved. No new contribution to this publication may be reproduced, stored in a retrieval system, or transmitted, in any form or by any means, electronic, mechanical, photocopying, recording, or otherwise, without the prior permission of the Publisher.

Cover Design Tiziana Matarazzo

Printed in the United States of America On 100% Acid-Free Paper

LITTLE BLUE BOOK NO. 1188
Edited by E. Haldeman-Julius

Sex and the Garden of Eden Myth

A Collection of Essays on Christianity

Maynard Shipley

HALDEMAN-JULIUS PUBLICATIONS
GIRARD, KANSAS

Copyright, 1927,
Haldeman-Julius Company

CONTENTS

Page
The Origin of Christianity................... 3
The Meaning of the Eucharist...............12
Pythagorean Sources of Certain
    Christian Doctrines 20
The Garden of Eden Myth in Its
    Relation to Sex Education................35
Christian Doctrines in Pre-Christian
    America 44
Debating the Fundamentalists..............61

PRINTED IN THE UNITED STATES OF AMERICA

SEX AND THE GARDEN OF EDEN MYTH

THE ORIGIN OF CHRISTIANITY

It is popularly believed that the religion known as Christianity was brought to the world either through the incarnation of Deity in the person of an only-begotten son, Jesus Christ, or by the teachings of a great spiritual leader, who was born at Nazareth in the reign of Augustus and died on the cross during the reign of Tiberius.

The four Gospels and the Acts of the Apostles are commonly understood to contain a genuine historical record of the life and teachings of this Hebrew "Redeemer" (Messiah) or Prophet. In short, it is widely accepted as an established fact that before the year 1 A. D., there was no Church corresponding to what is now known as Christian; no set of writings corresponding to (or forming the basis of) what is now known as the New Testament.

As a matter of fact, any scholar who has devoted any time to this subject knows that all these assumptions are incorrect. He knows that there were already in use a Gospel (known to the early Fathers of the Christian Church as "*the Diegesis*"), and an "Acts of the Apostles," both of which were old before the alleged immaculate conception of Nazareth; that all of the institutions and doctrines of what is now known as the Roman Catholic Church (and the orthodox Protestant Churches arising out of it) were already ancient in the days of

Augustus and Tiberius; and that the *only new conception* introduced by the Christian Church was the idea, attributed by them to "Jesus of Nazareth," that the end of the world was imminent—a matter of but a few months or years.

Just as Luther broke away from the Mother Church of Rome, so the Christian Church in the beginning was based upon the established Mother Church of the *Therapeutae* (or *Essenes*) of Alexandria, Egypt.

The cult of Jesus, in turn, was far more ancient than the Church of Alexandria, harking back to the primitive Joshua-Jesus sun-myth of remote antiquity. The "Gospel" of the Alexandrian Church was based largely upon a ritualistic or mystery play, a symbolical drama, whose origin it is difficult to trace with any degree of certainty.

To the authors of "the Gospel" and "the Acts," Jesus was not a known personality, but a *Name*—albeit a name to conjure with. Through employment of "the *Name*," demons, the cause of most diseases, were exorcised. The members of the original church were, therefore, a body of spiritual healers (*Therapeutae*, in Greek, *Essenes* in Egyptian—later "Christians").

Persons were "saved"—i. e., *cured*—by invocation of "the Name." I. E. S. U. S. (Jesus) possessed a greater magical (curative) power —so it was asserted—than, let us say, *Abracadabra*, or *Abraxas*: "There is none other Name under heaven given among men, whereby we must be saved" (Acts of the Apostles, iv, 12).

GARDEN OF EDEN MYTH 5

Some ailments, it was admitted, could not be cured (that is, the demons could not be driven out) by the invocation of "the Name" alone: "this kind goeth not out but by prayer and fasting" (Matt. xviii, 21).

Diseases (possession by demons, or "devils"), were often incurred by Black Magic (*Necromancy*), one or more demons taking abode in the victim's body, causing fever, insanity, or what not. The "Christians," following the Therapeutae of Egypt, practiced White Magic (*Leucomancy*), by which "evil spirits" were driven out by aid of "the Name"; or, in more stubborn cases of possession, by fastings and prayers, baptisms, sacraments, etc. These "remedies" were supposed to have the same efficacy over God himself that Black Magic had over evil demons and their supreme ruler, Satan.

To this day Christians (unknowingly adherents of the doctrine of the Therapeutae), both Roman Catholics and Protestants, *pray* for rain; for the cure of sick persons; and even for the release of the souls of the dead from the grip of the Devil (or of demons).

The sacred writings of the Gospel are still believed in some countries to possess magical influence, "as a spell of God," to drive away disease. "The Irish peasantry still continue to tie passages of St. John's Spell, or St. John's God's Spell, to the horns of cows to make them give more milk; nor would any power of rational argument shake their conviction of the efficacy of a bit of *the word*, tied round a colt's heels to prevent them from swelling"

(Rev. Robert Taylor). Sensible stablemen keep the stalls clean, and thus do away with the *cause* of the swelling; or do not permit their horses to wander too long in a bog.

Only the other day an editorial in a Fundamentalist journal complained that the health officer of the locality (in a southern state) closed up the churches to prevent further spread of an epidemic disease. It was argued that the churches should have been left open for the God-fearing people to assemble and pray for the heavenly suppression of the disease. These people are *real* Christians—true followers of the original Therapeutae of Egypt.

True healing, according to original Christian doctrine, comes from heaven, by divine agency. This was the conception of all ancient peoples. Even modern physicians still place the talismanic R (the mystical hieroglyph of Jupiter) at the beginning of a prescription. One must still have "faith" in the herb administered if good results are to be obtained. Christian Scientists omit the "herb" altogether, since all cures are really "by the same Spirit" (I Cor. xii).

"The miraculous powers which the Christians possessed," Father Origen assures us, "were not in the least owing to enchantments, but to their pronouncing the *name* I. E. S. U. S." This *name* had such power over the demons which produced the symptoms which we call "disease," "insanity," etc., that "it has sometimes proved effectual even though pronounced by very wicked persons" (Answer to Celsus, Chap. VI). We read of "vagabond Jews, exorcists, who took upon them to call over them which had evil spirits, the name of the Lord Jesus" (Acts xix, 13):—i. e., members of some competing healing sect.

Many persons suppose that the healings so often spoken of in the New Testament were made merely to prove that Jesus was verily the Son of God—the Messiah—and that the power was passed on to his disciples to be used in proving them to be especially empowered from heaven as healers, incidental to their function as founders of a new religion. This idea is wholly erroneous. They were professional *doctors, healers,* competing with other divine healers—"wicked persons," who dared attempt to break the monopoly of the original Egyptian apostles, graduates of the Alexandrian monastery, of which Jesus himself was reputed to have been a member (John, xvii, 16).*

St. Paul was himself a member of the Egyptian Ascetic order of Therapeutae, but, apparently, had become a seceder when his Epistles were written. His Epistles to the Colossians, to the Ephesians, and to Timothy, were directed against members of the Alexandrian College, the "Mother Church," with its strict discipline, and overbearing hierarchy—bishops and deacons "reigning in the plenitude of their distinctive authorities," yet needing, at times, to be admonished to be "not self-

---

*The correct reading of verse 2 of the fourteenth chapter of John is: "In my father's house are many places to be alone"—cells for the undisturbed reflection of solitary hermits. An *ascetic* would have no longing for a *mansion.*

willed, not given to wine, no strikers, and not given to filthy lucre" (Tit. i, 7).

There is strong evidence in support of the thesis that the exploits of the so-called "Jesus of Nazareth" were a compound of the ancient Joshua sun-myth and the story of the Indian Chrishna, "incarnate Deity of the Sanskrit Romance." Chrishna may have been the reputed (imaginary) founder of the Therapeutan monastery of Alexandria:

> What had been said to have been done in India, could be as well said to have been done in Palestine. The change of names and places, and the mixing up of various sketches of the Egyptian, Phœnician, Greek and Roman mythology, would constitute a sufficient disguise to evade the languid curiosity of infant skepticism. . . . The *probability* that that sect of vagrant quack-doctors, the Therapeutæ, who were established in Egypt and its neighborhood many ages before the period assigned by later theologians as that of the birth of Christ, were the original fabricators of the writings contained in the New Testament, becomes *certainty* on the basis of evidence, . . . unqualified and positive, . . . of the historian Eusebius, that *"those ancient Therapeutae were Christians, and their ancient writings were our Gospels and Epistles"* (Taylor, *The Diegesis*, pp. 63-64.)

This admission on the part of the great orthodox Church historian, Eusebius, Bishop of Caesarea, was by way of a "slip," in an unguarded moment; all the more unfortunate for some good souls, inasmuch as it is now well known that the Epistles were *written* long before the *original* Gospel (now lost, on which our present Gospels are based), and that both were written before the Jesus of the orthodox Christians was supposed to have been born.

The New Testament, as we have it now, was compiled by unknown persons, long after the time of the original reputed apostles or their companions, and is admittedly only "according to" the original writers. Even when first written, an old and highly complex ecclesiastical system was already flourishing, as even a cursory reading of the Epistles as they exist today clearly shows. As for the Gospels, the names of Pontius Pilate, Herod, Archelaus, Caiaphas, etc., along with numerous episodes, have been taken bodily from the works of Josephus, and substituted for the originals, which were not of Palestine, or else were of a much earlier period.

The Gospels as we have them were written by men who, though they may have been descended from Hebrews, knew little about the geography, history, chronology or statistics of Judea. In short, they were first written by the Therapeutan monks of Alexandria, before the Age of Augustus, and later tampered with by the early Christian writers.

In his reply to the arguments put forward by St. Augustine, the learned Manichean Christian and bishop, Faustus, said:

> For many things have been inserted by your ancestors in the speeches of our Lord, which, though put forth under His name, agree not with His faith; especially since—as already it has been often proved by us—these things were not written by Christ, nor by His apostles, but a long while after their assumption, by I know not what sort of half-Jews, not even agreeing with themselves, who made up their tale out of reports and opinions merely; and yet, fathering the whole upon the names of the apostles of the Lord, or on those who were supposed to have followed the apostles,

they mendaciously pretended that they had written their lies and conceits *according* to them (Faustus, Book 33, Chap. III).

As proof that what we now call the Christian religion was well established before the time of the reputed birth of Jesus of Nazareth, we have the testimony of Philo Judaeus, of Alexandria, a member of the order of Essenes, or Therapeutae, of that Egyptian city; who wrote an account of this sect, before Josephus, at the time when Jesus Christ could have been not above ten years of age, and at least fifty years before the existence of *any* extant Christian writing.

Philo's description of the institutions of the Therapeutae credited by Eusebius, shows that, in his time, this sect had established *churches* throughout the country; that each *parish* had its own temple and a *monastery;* that there were also bishops, priests, and deacons. The familiar Christian festivals of today were then regularly celebrated. The Therapeutae claimed to have had *apostolic* founders, who were not different in their practices from the apostles reputed to have followed the Christ of our New Testament. The priests of this sect used Scriptures which they believed to have been divinely inspired, and which Eusebius himself confessed were virtually the substance of our Gospels.

The Therapeutae employed the same allegorical method of interpreting their "sacred scriptures" which has since obtained among Christians generally, and their manner and order of performing public worship was the same as that seen in the churches of today. They established missionary communities in Rome, Corinth, Galatia, Ephesus, Philippi, Colossae and Thessalonica; "precisely such, and in such circumstances, as those addressed by St. Paul, . . . answering to every circumstance described of the state and discipline of the first community of Christians, *to the very letter*, . . . all this was nothing new in Philo's time, but of *then* long-established notoriety and venerable antiquity."

The writings contained in the New Testament are thus clearly shown to have been the accepted "sacred scriptures" of the Therapeutan monks *before* the Age of Augustus; and it becomes perfectly clear that what we now call orthodox Christianity is but a slightly modified form of the ancient religion of the Alexandrian Therapeutae — Essenes — Divine healers — Ascetics — Eclectics — Ecclesiastics — all names for one and the same sect, now known as "Christians."

And just as we discover in the religion of the Therapeutae of Egypt—described in detail by Eusebius Pamphilius, in the sixteenth chapter of the second book of his *Ecclesiastical History*—the Mother Church of the Christians, so do we find today most of the "customs of the ancients"—though "after a more Jewish fashion"—in both religions. The Christians of the second, third and fourth centuries made no attempt to hide the fact that their doctrines, rites, ceremonies, liturgies, etc., were essentially of pagan origin. On the contrary, they boasted that the pagan religion, *properly explained*, was really Christianity! And they did not hesitate to adduce data to demonstrate the essential identity of Paganism and Christianity.

To this day not more than one single notion or idea — the end-of-the-world delusion — can be shown to be *peculiar* to orthodox Fundamentalist Christianity. As for the Atoning Savior—"the Church's one foundation" of Fundamentalism—hear this from the *Prometheus Bound* of Aeschylus (acted at Athens 500 years before the Christian era):

> Lo, streaming from the fated tree,
>   His all-atoning blood!
> Is this the Infinite? 'Tis he—
>   Prometheus, and a God!
> Well might the sun in darkness hide,
>   And veil his glories in,
> When God, the great Prometheus, died,
>   For man, the creature's, sin.

THE MEANING OF THE EUCHARIST

On June 17, 1926, Roman Catholics from all parts of the earth—hundreds of thousand of them—gathered to eat their God: not symbolically, as do the Methodists, Baptists, Holy Rollers, etc., but *literally!* And why not? Did not Saint John the Divine state that Jesus of Nazareth, the incarnated Christian God, said: "Verily, verily I say unto you, Except ye eat the flesh of the Son of Man, and drink his blood, ye have no life in you. Whoso eateth my flesh, and drinketh my blood, shall have eternal life; ... He that eateth my flesh, and drinketh my blood, dwelleth in me, and I in him" (John vi, 53-56)?

So it has always been since the dawn of history. Men have always eaten their gods. In the oldest traditions of antiquity we find peoples eating—on special occasions—their totems or their gods—sometimes even their heroes!

The early Christians took over "the holy sacrament" (or *mysteries*) directly from the Pagans in whose midst they dwelt; and, in particular, the Eleusinian Mysteries of the Athenians, among whom "the Lord's supper" was the most solemn and august of all heathen sacraments.

Those holy mysteries were celebrated by the Athenians, at Eleusis, a town of Attica, and by many other Pagan peoples. The Lord's Supper was still being celebrated by various Pagan sects down to the last quarter of the fourth century, when, under the Inquisition set up by Theodosius I (the Great), all assemblies of non-Christians were declared unlawful, and all heathen temples were overthrown throughout the whole world. [Other edicts forbade even unorthodox Christians to hold meetings.]

Comparison of the Eleusinian Mysteries with the Christian sacrament shows clearly that the latter was derived directly from the former. For example:

Eleusinian Mysteries

1. But as the benefit of initiation was great, such as were convicted of witchcraft, murder, even though unintentional, or other heinous crimes, were debarred

Christian Sacrament

1. For as the benefit is great, if, with a true penitent heart and lively faith, we receive that holy sacrament . . . if any be an open and notorious evil - doer, or

from those mysteries.—
Bell's *Pantheon.*

2. At their entrance, purifying themselves by washing their hands in holy water, they were at the same time admonished to present themselves with pure minds, without which the external cleanness of the body would by no means be accepted.

3. The priests who officiated at these solemnities were called Hierophants, or *revealers of holy things.*

4. After this, they were dismissed in these words: "The Lord be with you."

hath done wrong to his neighbor, . . . that he presume not to come to the Lord's table.—Communion Service.

2. See the fonts of holy water at the entrance of every Roman Catholic Church in Christendom:
"Let us draw near with a true heart, having our hearts sprinkled from an evil conscience, and our bodies washed with pure water." (Heb. x, 22.)

3. "Let a man so account of us as of the ministers of Christ, and stewards of the mysteries of God." (I Cor. iv, 1.)

4. "The Lord be with you."

Among the Athenians these holy mysteries were celebrated in honor of Demeter, the goddess of corn, who, in allegorical language, had given us *her flesh to eat;* as Dionysus, the god of wine, had given us *his blood to drink.* (So Jesus said: "I am the true *vine* . . . As the branch cannot bear fruit of itself, except it abide in the *vine*, no more can you, except ye abide in me" (John xv, 1, 5).

Says the Rev. Dr. Robert Taylor (Diegesis, p 213, ed. of 1834):

If it were possible to be mistaken in the significancy of the monogram of Bacchus [Dionysus], the I H S, to whose honor, in conjunction with Ceres [Demeter], these holy mysteries were distinctively dedicated, the insertion of those letters in a circle of rays of glory, over the center of the holy table, is an hieroglyphic that depends not on the fallibility of translation, but conveys a sense that cannot be misread by any eye on which the sun's light shines. I H S are Greek characters, by ignorance taken for Roman letters; and YES, which is the proper reading of those letters, is none other than the very identical name of Bacchus, that is, of the Sun, of which Bacchus was one of the most distinguished personifications; and *Yes*, or *Ies*, with the Latin termination US added to it, is *Jesus*. The surrounding rays of glory, as expressive of the sun's light, make the identity of Christ and Bacchus as clear as the sun. These *rays of glory* are a sort of universal *letter* that cannot be misread or misinterpreted; no written language, no words that man could utter, could so distinctly, so expressively say that it was the Sun, and nothing but the Sun, that was so emblemized. And these rays are seen alike surrounding the heads of the Indian Chreeshna [Chrishna], as he is exhibited in the beautiful plate engraved by Barlow, and inscribed to the Archbishop of Canterbury; round the Grecian Apollo; and in all our pictures of Jesus Christ. . . . The Sun and the Lord were perfectly synonymous, and *Sun's day* and *the Lord's day* the same to every nation on whom his light hath shone.

Doane (Bible Myths, p 351, ed. 1882) says, in this connection:

Even the charm which is worn by the Christians at the present day, has none other than the monogram of Bacchus engraved thereon, i. e., I H S. [Falsely supposed to stand for *Jesus Hominum Salvator*, or *In Hoc Signo*.] It is none other than the identical monogram of the heathen god Bacchus, and was to be seen on the coins of the Maharajah of Cashmere.

Dr. Inman says (Ancient Faiths, Vol. 1, pp. 518-519):

For a long period I H S, I E E S, was a monogram of Bacchus, letters now adopted by the Romanists. Hesus was an old divinity of Gaul, possibly left by the Phœnicians. We have the same I H S in Jezebel, and reproduced in our Isabel.

The idea connected with the word is *"Phallic Vigor."*

The god Bacchus—*Io Nisso* (O Lord, direct us!), from which the Greeks derived Dionysus—appears in nearly all the religions of antiquity under one name or another—always as the Sun-God. In Egypt he was Osiris, in India Dionysus, and "not improbably Chrishana, as he was called Adoneus, which signified the Lord of Heaven, or the Lord and Giver of Light, in Arabic; and Liber, throughout the Roman dominions, from whence is derived our term *liberal*, for everything that is generous, frank, and amiable"—and *tolerant*. Orpheus states that Bacchus was a lawgiver, and attributes to him the two tables of the law.

It was, then, especially in honor of the universal Sun-God, Bacchus, called by Horace "the modest God," "the decent God," that the *mysteries* were celebrated by bread and wine—the Lord's supper. I H S, the ancient monogram of the Sun, is now seen in Catholic Churches as the monogram of the Sun-God Christ Jesus.

Bacchus, so the story goes, was the "Only Begotten Son" (Knight, *Ancient Art and Mythology*, p. xxii, note) of Zeus and Demeter (Jupiter and Semele). Desiring that his son should be the "Slain one," "Sin Bearer" (Bonwick, *Egyptian Belief*, p. 169), and "Redeemer" of the world (Dupuis, *Origin of Religious Beliefs*, p. 135), Jupiter "overshadowed" the beautiful young virgin, who became the mother of the Savior-God Bacchus. An inscription on a monument to Bacchus reads: "It is I (says the Lord Bacchus to mankind) who guides you; it is I who protects you, and who saves you; I am Alpha and Omega" (Higgins, *Anacalypsus*, Vol. I, p. 130).

Charles F. Dupuis, describing the "holy mysteries" or rites of Bacchus, says (*Traite des Mysteres*, ch. I):

The sacred doors of the Temple in which the initiation took place were opened only once a year, and no stranger might ever enter. . . . It was the sole occasion for the representation of the passion of Bacchus dead, descended into hell, and re-arisen—in imitation of the representation of the sufferings of Osiris which, according to Herodotus, were commemorated at Sais in Egypt. It was in that place that the partition of *the body of the god*, which was then eaten—the ceremony, in fact, of which our Eucharist is only a reflection; whereas in the mysteries of Bacchus actual raw flesh was distributed, which each of those present had to consume in commemoration of the death of Bacchus dismembered by the Titans, and whose passion, in Chios and Tenedos, was renewed each year by the sacrifice of a man who represented the god.

If we are to believe the Christian authors, it was Jesus of Nazareth who instituted the Eucharist. Unfortunately for their claims, as we have seen, this *mystery* of breaking bread and drinking of wine—the natural body and blood of Christ Jesus *vere et realiter*, according to Roman Catholics—is of very ancient origin, and is recorded, as I have said, in the history of practically all religions, in the Americas as well as in the Old World. The Chinese pour wine—a universal substitute for blood—on a straw image of Confucius, and then communicants drink of it, and taste the "sacrificed victim" in order to participate in the grace of Confucius. (Read here again the New Testament version.)

Williamson (*The Great Law of Religious Origins*, p. 177, 1899) tells us that the ancient Egyptians "celebrated the resurrection of Osiris by a sacrament, eating the sacred cake or wafer after it had been consecrated by the priest, and thereby becoming veritably flesh of his flesh." The adherents of the Grand Lama in Thibet and Tartary offer to their god a sacrament of bread and wine (Higgins, *Anacalypsus*, Vol. I, p. 232, and Vol. II, p. 118). The ancient Mexicans celebrated "the most holy supper" much as do the modern Christians. (See an article by the present writer, "Christian Doctrines in Pre-Christian America," *Haldeman-Julius Monthly*, April, 1926.)

"Among the ancient Hindoos," says Baring-Gould, "Soma was a chief deity; he is called 'the Giver of Life and of Health,' the 'Protector,' he who is 'the Guide to Immortality.' He became incarnate among men, was taken by them and slain, and brayed in a mortar. But he rose in flames to heaven, to be the 'Benefactor of the World,' and the 'Mediator between God and Man.' Through communion with him in his sacrifice, man (who partook of the god) has an assurance of immortality, for by that *sacrament* he obtains union with his divinity" (*Origins of Religious Belief*, Vol. I, p. 401).

Cicero (106-43 B. C.) mentions the Eucharist as a strange rite: "How can a man be so stupid as to imagine that which he eats to be a god?"

Doane remarks (*Bible Myths*, pp. 314-315):

It was many centuries before the genuine heathen doctrine of *Transubstantiation*—a change of the elements of the Eucharist into the *real* body and blood of Christ Jesus — became a tenet of the Christian faith. This greatest of mysteries was developed gradually. As early as the second century, however, the seeds were planted, when we find Ignatius, Justin Martyr and Irænæus advancing the opinion that the mere bread and wine became, in the Eucharist, *something higher*—the earthly, something heavenly — without, however, ceasing to be bread and wine. Though these views were opposed by some eminent individual Christian teachers, yet both among the people and in the ritual of the Church, the miraculous or supernatural view of the Lord's Supper gained ground. After the third century the office of presenting the bread and wine came to be confined to the ministers or priests. The practice arose from, and in time strengthened, the notion which was gaining ground, that in the act of presentation by the priest, a sacrifice, similar to that once offered up in the death of Christ Jesus, though bloodless, was ever anew presented to God. This still deepened the feeling of the *mysterious* significance and importance with which the rite of the Lord's Supper was viewed, and led to that gradually increasing splendor of celebration which took the form of the *Mass*. . . . For a long time there was no formal declaration of the mind of the Church on the *real presence* of Christ Jesus in the Eucharist. . . . At the present day, the Greek and Roman Catholics alone hold to the original doctrine of the real presence—a view, however, upheld by Calvin.

The cannibalistic connotations of the Eucharistic phraseology did not escape the challenge of Pagan philosophers. The reply of the Fathers was that the terms were purely figurative. Such was the doctrine taught by Augustine. But when Pagan culture had been crushed under the iron heel of the Church, and there were no thinkers left to challenge the Church as such, there remained no further difficulty in establishing the barbarous doctrine that "what was eaten in the Eucharist was by 'transubstantiation' the actual flesh and blood of the God-Man."

"Where such a belief was possible," remarks J. M. Robertson (*A Short History of Christianity*, p. 189, 1913), "it was the special interest of the priesthood to make the affirmation. A stupendous miracle, they claimed, was worked every time the Eucharist was administered; but it was worked through the priest. . . . Under such a dominating conception, Christianity was for the majority a religion neither of faith nor works; it was a system of sacerdotal magic. . . . He only that received the mystic rite at consecrated hands was to be saved. . . . The rite [now called the *missa* or Mass—the formula of dismissal, *"Ite, missio est,"* corrupted into *"Missa est"*] was developed by the addition of chants and responses till it became the special act of Christian worship."

This rite is now the basis of the moral power of the Roman Catholic Church.

It is this age-old, pre-Christian, heathen "mystery" which brought so many deluded victims of superstition to the great city of Chicago in this so-called Age of Reason.

PYTHAGOREAN SOURCES OF CERTAIN CHRISTIAN DOCTRINES

Christianity being based upon purely Pagan religious rites, ceremonies and beliefs, and more directly upon the Eclectic Philosophy of the Egyptian Essenes or Therapeutae—"Healers," "Doctors"—we are not surprised to find numerous elements of the Pythagorean doctrine in the Acts of the Apostles and the Four Gospels, the "Sage of Samos" being one of their most revered Masters. One might, however, be surprised to learn how much of the teaching commonly ascribed to Jesus Christ is really the prior teaching of Pythagoras, the greatest of the earlier Greek philosophers, whose writings carry us back to the sixth century B. C.

Pythagoras, in turn, was the most distinguished pupil of the theologian Pherecydes, of Syros, who was, according to Cicero and Augustine, the first philosopher to inculcate the doctrine of the distinct existence and immortality of the soul, and who was certainly the first European exponent of the doctrine of metempsychosis, a theory which we find embodied in the "Orphic mysteries," celebrated especially at Athens.

Orphism and Pythagoreanism were both schools of eclectic philosophy, their adherents adopting the best features of all philosophies and religious systems. Thus we find in the New Testament "a collection of all the diverging rays of truth which were scattered through the various systems of Pagan and Jewish piety," brought to one brilliant focus of "whatsoever things are of good report"—characteristic Pythagorean doctrine, summarized in Paul's Epistle to the Philippians (iv, 8). So with the famous "Golden Rule," which we owe, not to the Jews or to the Christians, but to the Chinese *via* the missionary Therapeutæ.

It can hardly be doubted, in view of their fame as extensive travelers (missionaries), that the members of the Therapeutan order had visited China, as well as India, Persia, Greece, Italy, etc. As these ascetic monks, or Eclectics were avowedly collectors and adopters of the best tenets of moral and religious philosophy which they could anywhere find, it is quite possible—even probable—that the Golden Rule found in our New Testament had its origin in China, since it is known that the great Chinese emperor Kon-futz-see (Confucius) had given expression to the same rule about 500 years before the date assigned for the birth of the Christ of the Gospels.

This Chinese maxim, "Do unto others as you would that they should do unto you," was adopted into the Moral Gnomologue, "or put into the mouth of the Demon of the Diegesis, from whence it passed into the copies of epitomes of the Diegesis, which have been falsely taken for the original composition of Matthew, Mark and Luke" (Taylor, *The Diegesis*, p. 244).

In an English edition of Kon-futz-see by Josephus Tela (reprinted from an edition of 1691), the 24th Maxim of Confucius is thus translated:

"Do to another what you would that he should do to you, and do not unto another what you would not should be done unto you. Thou only needst this law alone. It is the foundation and principle of all the rest." This is summarized in Matthew vi, 12: "Therefore, all things whatsoever ye would that men should do unto you, do ye even so to them; for this is the law and the prophets."

Taylor, on the basis of universally accepted canons of criticism, considers that we must regard the abridged form and more smoothly constructed sentence, "the later composition, consequently the plagiarism."

Is it not significant that Pythagoras, and, centuries later, Plato (in the fourth century B. C.), in their quest for knowledge—"truth"—visited, not the Jews, but the Egyptians, Hindus, Persians, Babylonians and Phœnicians?

It was the Pythagoreans—including the monastic precursors of the Christians, known as the Therapeutæ of Alexandria—who "were the possessors of all the sciences known in their time"—geometry, astronomy, music, physics and medicine.

Yet the Christian apologist, Lactantius, hypocritically wonders why they should never have consulted the Jews! (*Divin. Inst.*, Bk. IV, Chap. 2).

As a matter of fact, the Jews had nothing new or original to offer in the way of either science or "truth." To visit them in the quest for knowledge would have been to seek secondhand information when first-hand sources were as readily accessible. Before the Hebrews had themselves visited Egypt, Assyria and Babylonia—in the capacity of slaves—they were but barbarians, victims of crass ignorance and superstition.

But the Hebrews, nevertheless, had a certain genius all their own, and were never without men of potential greatness; and their leaders and thinkers did not fail to absorb and make their own all the knowledge made available to them by their enforced travels and sojourns in the civilized countries by whose rulers they were successively defeated and enslaved. In the course of centuries, especially during the period of and immediately following the Babylonian Captivity, the priests of Judah, studious, thoughtful and acquisitive, attained the distinction of being the most voracious and successful plagiarists of antiquity.

"Eclectics" in practice, they cleverly disguised their appropriated knowledge and ideas in typical Hebrew literary forms, boldly presenting them to the world as original contributions of Jewish lore and wisdom—admixed, albeit, with genuine Hebraic poetry and literature of a very high order.

So today, we have a so-called Jewish "sacred scriptures," from Genesis to Malachi, made up mostly of the laws, legends, philosophy, folk-lore, and wisdom of the civilized peoples of antiquity—drawn freely, and in many cases undisguisedly, from Babylonian, Chaldean, Assyrian, Persian, Egyptian, Phœnician, Indian and Grecian sources. Verily, the Bible is indeed "the Book of Books"!

While Hebraic legends and poetry are frequently referred to or quoted in the New Testament, its doctrine of the immortality of the soul and metempsychosis is of non-Jewish origin, and, so far as Europe and the Near East were concerned, was of Greek source, appearing first in the Orphic rites of the Athenian Eleusinian Mysteries.

In the Orphic "mysteries" the soul was regarded as a prisoner in the mortal body, and *redemption* meant escape from the earth-life, to which the immortal soul had been doomed by sins in a former existence. The soul may attain perfection by metempsychosis, or transmigration from one body to another, in a series of reincarnations. This doctrine was inculcated by Pythagoras, and adopted by the Essenes, or Therapeutæ, of Egypt. Through the latter it became, as we shall see, part of the "teachings of Jesus."

Pythagoras, like so many wise and exalted characters of pre-Christian days, served as a model of the supernatural Jesus Christ of the Augustan Age. As in the case of the Jewish Messiah (Christ) of Christianity, Pythagoras was "the object of a splendid dispensation of prophecy, and had his birth foretold by Apollo Pythus," hence his name *Pyth-agoras*.*

His disciples regarded the soul of the great Master as having been descended from a "primeval state of companionship with the divine Apollo." The same was said of all the "only begotten" sons of the gods of antiquity. "And the Word was made flesh and dwelt among us (and we beheld his glory, the glory as of the only begotten of the Father), full of grace and truth" (John i, 14).

The Alexandrian Greek author (or authors)

---

*Latona, mother of Apollo by the supreme deity Jupiter—never having "known" men—was persecuted all her life by the dragon Python. The Greeks referred to Apollo as "our Lord and Savior Phœbus Apollo," who possessed "the brightness of his father's glory" and "the express image of his person." The son of the Father-God (Jupiter) at length slew his mother's persecutor, and was thereupon "exalted with great triumph unto his kingdom in heaven": and the seed of the woman bruised the serpent's head, "and her child was caught up to God and to His throne" (Rev. xii, 5).

of the Fourth Gospel speak of "the glory which he had with the Father before the world was" (John vii, 5).

Scholars are not wanting who regard Pythagoras as the greatest moral teacher of antiquity; "the most clear and unquestionable type of the character afterwards set forth to the world under the *prosopoeia* [abstract person] generally designated as Jesus Christ."

The immortal Plato acknowleged his great indebtedness to the teachings of the Pythagoreans; and the Alexandrian founders of Christianity, compilers and revisers of the old Acts and the Gospel—known to them as *Diegesis*—show plainly the Platonic sources of much of their "inspiration."

With the foregoing facts in mind, it is to be anticipated that the Gospels and the Acts strongly reflect not only Platonic doctrine, but also that of the exalted teachings of the Samian sage, "first of philosophers," and "teacher of the purest system of morals ever propounded to man."

The Egyptian Therapeutæ proudly claimed Pythagoras as a member of their monastic institution, and to him is ascribed their practice of holding all property in common: "as many as were possessors of lands or houses, sold them, and brought the prices of the things that were sold, and laid them down at the apostles' feet; and distribution was made to every man according as he had need" (Acts iv, 34-35).

To Pythagoras, as I have stated, is due the acceptance of the doctrine of metempsychosis (transmigration of souls) by the Therapeutæ.

"As much as this doctrine is now scouted," says the learned Godfrey Higgins, "it was held not only by almost all the great men of antiquity," but "it was fully accepted by the early Christian Fathers, and later by several sects of Christians" (*Celtic Druids*, pp. 283 ff.). Some of the later Christians, however, rejected this ancient doctrine, as it seemed to them to deprive them of their comforting belief in eternal torment in hell's fires for persons who were wickedly opposed to their own views.

"The Christian doctrine of original sin, and of the necessity of being *born again*," says Taylor (*The Diegesis*, p. 220), are evident misunderstandings of the doctrine of the Pythagorean Metempsychosis, which constituted the inward spiritual grace, or essential significancy of the Eleusinian mysteries; as the classical reader will find those mysteries sublimely treated of in the sixth book of Virgil's Æneid. The term of migration, during which the soul of man was believed to expiate in other forms the deeds done in its days of humanity, was exactly *a thousand* years; after which, drinking of the waters of Lethe, which caused a forgetfulness of all that had passed, it was ferried down the river, or sailed under the conduct of Mercury, the *Logos* or *Word of God*, and, 'wind and tide serving,' was so borne or carried, and *born of water and wind* [rendered "born of water and of the spirit" in John iii, 5, but properly translated, "born of the wind"], and launched into humanity, for a fresh experiment of moral probation."

The real meaning of *born in sin* relates not

to a literal "Fall of Man," but to souls that "had acquitted themselves but ill in a previous existence." According to this doctrine, the soul would again come into the world bringing the results of "a corrupt nature," as the result of maladjusted—"sinful"—conduct in its previous existence. Further difficulties would need to be overcome as a discipline or preparation for ultimate achievement of that happiness which is the natural reward of right conduct, or "virtue." Thus, "Jesus answered and said unto him, verily, I say unto thee, except a man be born again [and again?] he cannot see the kingdom of heaven" (John iii, 3).

Jesus is revealed in the New Testament as preeminently a teacher of this ancient doctrine. All wise men were assumed to be acquainted with it. Hence Christ's rebuke of the Jewish rabbi Nicodemus: "Art thou a Master of Israel, and knowest not these things?" (John iii, 10). Jesus himself was frequently addressed as "Master"—a Pythagorean epithet.

If the reader will now turn to the New Testament and read it in the light of what has just been said, he will at once discover the Pythagorean elements in its teachings.

The term of migration during which the soul of man was to undergo its educative discipline, through the lessons of adversity and suffering, was as previously stated, a thousand years: "For a thousand years in thy sight are but as yesterday; seeing that is passed as a watch in the night." The forgetfulness of Lethe and rebirth: "Thou turnest men to destruction: again thou sayest, *Come again*, ye children of men'." [The evident quotation, which I have so remarked, being from some sacred scripture —*Word of God*—older than any of the Gospel documents known to us.]

The ninetieth Psalm, selected to be read as part of the burial service in the Church of England, is wholly Pythagorean, and is based upon the doctrine of metempsychosis, "the Lord" being "our refuge *from one generation to another.*"

Elias returns to the flesh for further spiritual development in the person of John the Baptist (Matt. xvii, 10-13)—a doctrine confirmed by Jesus himself—or by those theologians who created this imaginary "Christ" as an embodiment of their own beliefs. In the ninth chapter of Luke the question of the return of "the old prophets," or of "Elias," or of John the Baptist is twice mentioned—verses 7-9, and verses 18-21. To quote the latter:

"And it came to pass as he was *alone* praying, *his disciples were with him* (*sic!*): and he asked them, saying, Whom (*sic*) say the people that I am? They answering said, John the Baptist; but some say, Elias; and others say, that one of the old prophets is risen again. He said unto them, But who (*sic*) say ye that I am? Peter answering said, the Christ of God. And he straitly charged them, and commanded them to tell no man that thing."

It would seem that the original *Diegesis*, upon which the New Testament as we have it was founded, was clearer in its teachings as to the existence of disembodied souls, migrating from body to body, in successive reincarnations. At any rate, we read of Elias' having, perhaps, *risen* again, in his own body. The orthodox Christian believes in the resurrection of the *body* as well as in the immortality of the soul.

When Jesus departed for his reputed three-day sojourn in hell, his *body* was missing from the sepulchre. Pythagorean doctrine would leave the dead body where it was deposited, the immortal soul being a spirit, as "God is a spirit"; hence, having no need for a carnal body. This is also the Platonic conception of immortality.

To the orthodox Jew, a disembodied spirit was inconceivable. If one "returned" he returned in the flesh. The guerdon for right conduct in the Old Testament was that one might "live long" in the flesh, not as a gaseous "immortal spirit." The good man's hoped-for moral reward was that he should "prosper"—a reward measurable in terms of goats, sheep, camel, or shekels. The metaphysical rewards of Pythagoreanism would hardly appeal to the "hard-headed business man," either among the Jews or among the Gentiles. So the ethics and theology of the New Testament of the Christian Fathers is a compromise Gospel—often self-contradictory.

It is all but certain that the compilers of the New Testament, as we have it, omitted much of the exalted religious and ethical teachings of Pythagoras and the earlier Therapeutæ. For example, his tender respect for women, and generous insistence upon their rights, is given little emphasis in the Gospels; while Paul's teachings have ever been used by his most devout followers in their fight against the rights of women.

Among the Therapeutæ, women were recognized as *the equals of the males in all respects.* The views of Paul himself—a seceder from the Therapeutan order—are exemplified in I Corinthians xiv, 34, 45, and, again, in Ephesians v, 22-24; I Tim. ii, 11-14.

The cruelties to children and animals, here and there countenanced by the Old Testament writers, find no vindication in the Gospels even as we now have them. The humane teachings of Pythagoras had taken so deep a root in the consciousness of humanity, that even the seceding monks who invented the story of a Messiah of the Age of Augustus—thus bringing the older Jesus myth "down to date," so to speak— would not have dared to attempt the reintroduction of Old Testament ideas relative to the treatment of women and children.*

In an age of polytheism, Pythagoras stoutly maintained the monotheistic idea of the unity of God—who "is all in all" (I Cor. xv, 28)— and based his lofty moral precepts upon the brotherhood of man, extending his compassion and tenderness, as did the unknown author of

---

*For examples of these "Old Covenant" ideas, consult the following chapters and verses of "the Word of God": (*Women*) Gen. iii, 16; Ex. xxi, 7; Deut. xxi, 10-14; xxiv, 1; Judges xxi, 21; II Samuel xii, 11; Isaiah xiii, 16; Jer. xviii, 21; Zech. xiv, 2: (*Children*) Prov. xxiii, 14; Prov. xxix, 15; Deut. xxi, 16; xix, 21; Isaiah xiii, 16; Levit, xxvi, 22; II Samuel xii, 15, 18; II Kings ii, 23, 24; Ex. xx, 5; Hosea xiii, 16.

Ecclesiastes (iii, 19), to the whole brute creation: "all have one breath; so that a man hath no preeminence above a beast."*

He strongly protested against the cruelties and wickedness of war, as being, under all conditions contrary to the eternal obligations of moral virtue.

Declaring that "none but God is wise," Pythagoras recognized the virtue of humility and the folly of vanity, recommending constant self-examination as a corrective of swollen pride, and of the all too human tendency to look with scorn or contempt upon the foibles of our fellow man.

Charitable to a degree, yet exacting in its ethical demands, the greatest philosopher, mathematician and religious elder of his age fell at last a victim to the vengeance of one he could not recognize as eligible to the cooperative society of Crotona. Incensed by his rejection, and backed by the hostile local authorities, the unsuccessful applicant set fire to the house in which Pythagoras and his disciples were gathered—sixty of whom, including the Master, were devoured by the flames, while the rest of the monks—more than 200 of them—found safety in flight.

It has been suggested that this violent destruction of the colony at Crotona (in Magna Græcia, Italy), is the basis of the fabulous story detailed in the second chapter of the Acts

---

*"God is spirit" (John iv, 24), and "the spirit of the Lord is His breath" (II Thes. ii, 2).

of the Apostles, when the apostles "were all with one accord in one place," and the Holy Ghost descended, *in the form of fire*, upon their heads.

The "One Only God" of Pythagoras was by no means the anthropomorphic Deity of the ancient Jews and the modern Fundamentalists. "God," he taught, "is neither the object of sense, nor *subject to passion*, but invisible, only *intelligible*, and supremely intelligent. In his body he is *like* the light,* and in his soul he *resembles* truth. He is the universal spirit that pervades and diffuses itself over all nature. ["God *is* all and *in* all" (I Cor. xv, 28). On this thesis there can be no personal God.] *All* beings receive their life from him. There is but One Only God! who is not, as some are apt to imagine, seated above the world beyond the orb of the universe [as in "Our Father, which art in heaven," etc.]; but being himself *all in all,* he sees all the beings that fill his immensity, the *only principle*, the light of heaven, *the Father of all* ["I and my father are one"]. He produces everything, he orders and disposes of everything; he is the reason, the life, and the motion of all beings."

Compare this beautiful conception of Deity with the Jehovah of "the Word of God," worshiped by our modern Fundamentalists, and see how far we should have traveled under Pythagorean—"Pagan"—guidance! Here is a

---

*"God *is* light, and in him is no darkness at all" (John i, 5).

Biblical picture of Yahweh (Jehovah), the God of Abraham, of Isaac and of Jacob:

"Blessed be the Lord of my strength, which teacheth my hands to war, and my fingers to fight" (Psalms, cxliv, 1); and "cursed be he that keepeth back his sword from blood" (Jer. xlviii, 10). "The Lord thy God is a *jealous* God" (Ex. xxxiv, 14); knowing "fierce *anger*" (Num. xxv, 4), susceptible to *fear* (Deut. xxxii, 27), *grief* (Gen. vi, 6), *repentance* (Amos vii, 6), *hate* (Prov. vi, 27), *vindictiveness* (Rom. xii, 19), etc., etc. "Now go to Amalek, and utterly destroy all that they have, and spare them not; but slay both man and woman, infant and suckling, ox and sheep, camel and ass" (I Sam. xv, 3).

I should prefer the God of the "Pagan" Pythagoras! But this God, we may rest assured, would not require a system of salvation based upon a demand for the murder of his "only begotten son" to appease his own anger, and through whose sufferings the sins of others could be remitted. For the Pythagoreans, salvation—ethical evolution—was a personal matter, atonement for past sins being made by (educative) subsequent struggle for self-development, leading to the realization of some worthy ideal. This aspect of the Pythagorean teachings was minimized by the editors of the New Testament as we have it, and the atonement idea over-emphasized—a concession to Pagan superstition. This fact has long been recognized by the better educated clergy.

THE GARDEN OF EDEN MYTH IN ITS RELATION TO SEX EDUCATION

That the Fundamentalist view of the cosmos and man is essentially infantile and narcissistic is self-evident. Perhaps all aspects of obscurantism are equally so. During the past five years, doubtless as an aftermath of war hysteria, we have witnessed a remarkable recrudescence, or exaggeration, of the infantilism normally associated with religious fanaticism. As symptomatic of this psychologically regressive tendency, we note the unusual number of child preachers, or evangelists, who have stepped into the limelight amid the glad rejoicing of their elders of the same psychological age. Infantile themselves, the Stratons and Rileys and Sundays find the "message" of the child evangelists quite gratifying to their own self-love and child-like mentality.

The child evangelist and the Fundamentalist elder are possessed (or obsessed) by the same thoughts (phantasies) and feelings, the same fears and longings, the same subconscious—and repressed—desires; both live in an emotional dreamland; both love the fairy-tale view of life; both clothe their subconscious desires in objective symbols, and pretend they are bravely facing reality.

As is well known, religious emotion is more intense during adolescence than at any other period of life, because associated with awakening—and perhaps unwelcome—sex-consciousness. Religious mythology expresses itself in sexual symbolism because it springs from subconscious sexual disturbances, even in adults.

The Garden of Eden myth—known in one form or another among all ancient peoples, and the indispensable foundation of orthodox Christian theology—is an inevitable product of infantilism, or, in adults, of psychical regression. It is an expression of the universal human desire to "return to the mother," as has been amply demonstrated by Otto Rank (in *Das Traum der Geburt*), and, independently, by Cavendish Moxon, a leading psycho-analyst of San Francisco (*The Psycho-analytic Review*, July 1924). "When the interest in reality has hardly been maintained in early life," says Mr. Moxon, "there is a specially strong tendency after middle age to regress to a primitive psychical level."

The "forbidden fruit" of the Tree of Knowledge is not knowledge in general, as might be inferred, but pertains more largely to sexual knowledge by experience.

An intelligent interpretation of this universal myth of a lost Paradise is highly important from the viewpoint of the educator, the legislator, and the student of religious and social problems. Mr. Moxon, in particular, has made a most interesting and informative contribution to the literature of this subject; and, because his paper is not readily available to most readers, a brief summary of his discussion should prove of value.

Moreover, a correct analysis of the Genesis story has a direct bearing on the otherwise difficult problem of how much sexual enlightenment—if any—should be given the mentally inquisitive child. Unfortunately, not only the priest and the Fundamentalist preacher, but, often, even free-thinking parents are inclined (for reasons which they themselves do not understand) to disapprove of telling the truth in such matters to the young. Some self-styled "liberals" even contend that the ordinary adult citizen should not be informed of "what crude sexual impulses are directly expressed in the behavior of the child and savage." It is better, they assert, that the average man should not be taught that most of the religious symbols and mystical experiences of modern men and women are the direct expression of natural —but usually suppressed—sexual impulses. Such "liberal" conservatives are themselves in need of further enlightenment.

Clinging tenaciously (and the more tenaciously because subconsciously) as he does to the primitive and infantile state of "pleasant phantasy," the Fundamentalist, or often even the Modernist or Free-thinker, is averse to facing boldly and honestly the outer world of reality. The former has "little or no interest in the discovery of truth and the elimination of error." All Fundamentalists are of this psychical type or age. They are merely grown-up infants; or, in some cases, children. The average adult is more advanced in psychical age; hence he strives to adapt his impulses to the requirements of the external world. Self-love and infantile phantasy give way before the impulse to love objects in the world of outer reality. Curiosity, interest in natural phenomena, the desire for an understanding of natural processes, lead to the development of a scientific attitude toward life and its manifold expressions.

But while the reality principle holds a dominant place in the consciousness of the true scientist, nevertheless, even among men of science we find many individuals who, as Moxon puts it, "have an endless struggle against their tendency to choose such beliefs about the world as will enrich their imagination with lasting pleasure and comfort."

All men retain at least some traces of their primitive urge toward "an endless repetition of states of pleasant phantasy." The unconscious never forgets its longing for the peace of Paradise. "The organic involuntary process strengthens the desire found even in youthful mystics to return to such a primitive pleasure in rest and peace as that which preceded birth."

These basic principles not only give us the key to correct interpretation of the Garden of Eden myth, but they also enable us to understand the unconscious forces that act as resistances to the sexual enlightenment of the youth.

The priest, having renounced (theoretically at least) the pleasure of earthy love, and the parent, teacher or older person who is threatened by an unwelcome loss of power, alike tend to compensate for their loss by identification with the children to whom they stand in the relation of mentor. By "the mechanism of identification," the forces of self-love and child-love combine to form a resistance to scientific instruction in general and to sexual enlightenment in particular. Very often you will find among Fundamentalist objections to the teaching of evolution a hardly masked complaint that the child's "morals" as well as its "faith" will be endangered.

Moxon finds another unconscious cause of the prevalent resistance in parents, clergymen and teachers against the proper instruction of children in sex matters, in the envy and jealousy of the elders: "For to the unconscious, the young appear as dangerous rivals and revive in the elders the old fears and hates of their own rival parent in the nursery days. The discoveries of Freud have forced us to admit that, in addition to the tender consideration for the helpless, there are self-regarding and even hostile feelings toward the young behind such pleas for ignorance as that contained in Tennyson's lines:

> "Leave thou thy sister when she prays,
> Her early Heaven, her happy views;
> Nor thou with shadow'd hint confuse
> A life that leads melodious days."

In this connection it is interesting also to recall Ibsen's "Master Builder," and Solness' fear of "the young generation" who would come "knocking at the door."

Here we came upon the underlying *motif* of the Garden of Eden myth, the Paradise story being a vivid symbolization of the regressive ideas alluded to in the foregoing paragraphs. "The Garden of Eden myth in the book of Genesis," says Moxon, "vividly pictures the struggle between the conscious desire for psychosexual adulthood and the infantile forces of inertia. . . . Man and woman have the choice between an infantile life of narcissistic satisfaction of impulse in the enchanted garden and an adult life of sexual intercourse and cultural activity, with the pain involved in work and childbirth, in the world outside. In Paradise (the Mother), food flows to the body without effort; in the world outside food is obtained only by the sweat of the brow, and love involves sacrifice. The myth itself merely presents the psychological facts in symbolic form. The use that is made of it depends on the desires of the moralist who appeals to its authority. And it has been fateful for education that in the past this myth has been interpreted by persons who were largely dominated by an unconscious desire to return to the psychical conditions symbolized as Paradise. The elders, like the myth maker, yearned for the lost state of happiness where pain, work, and weakness were unknown and guilt was absent."

This lies also behind the Greek and Roman myth of the "Golden Age," the description of which corresponds to all the same criteria.

Desiring divine authority (parental approval) for the enjoyment of this self-centered, infantile, sheltered, irresponsible love-yearning, the Yahweh (Jehovah) symbol is projected. An awakened, fully developed (psychically adult) relation to life and its problems is regarded, not as a natural maturing of the individual into a higher and richer life—the life of reality—but as a "Fall" to a lower level of existence. Bliss is to be found only in "sinless ignorance"—the thought of Tennyson—his "melodious days." At its lowest level, from the viewpoint of the psycho-analyst, the psychical condition symbolized as Paradise is the womb of the mother. "If the Garden of Eden means the intrauterine life for which the phantasy of every man unconsciously longs, it follows that the expulsion from the Garden is a symbol of Birth into the outer world. Consequently the prohibition of sexual knowledge is not binding upon those who strive consciously to live psycho-sexual adulthood according to what Freud terms the adult principle."

At a higher level of the Paradise symbolism, we meet with the conflict implied between the son, Adam, and the father-substitute, Yahweh, for the possession of Eve, "the mother of all flesh." Jealous of Adam's emerging adulthood, the father prepares the Tree of Knowledge which bears forbidden fruit—knowledge and power to be gained by Adam through his sexual relationship with Eve. Yahweh resents the end of Adam's psycho-sexual infantilism in the father's house. The Edenic serpent symbolizes "man's libidinous desire which makes him rebel against a perpetual state of childhood dependence and sexual immaturity." The snake is, incidentally, a well recognized phallic emblem.

But psycho-sexual maturity involves mental adulthood, as well; hence the serpent becomes the symbol of man's urge for intellectual achievement, for adulthood not only as a lover but also in relation to the cultural life of art and science. "The static and regressive tendencies of the human being," says Moxon, "speak through the voice of Yahweh, who wills to keep mankind in ignorant dependence in Paradise. . . . The serpent, like Oedipus, represents the adult's scientific interest which grows out of sexual curiosity. . . . The sublimated libido of a serpent appears in the objective curiosity of the modern man of science who strives to construct a view of the world that is free from the distortions of infantile self-love. . . . At the cost of sadness and solitude, he is determined to know the facts about himself and his world and he will not leave the young in the Paradise of ignorant inactivity."

The infantile narcissism of the Fundamentalist makes his ego the center of the universe, which exists solely for the satisfaction of his needs, fancied or real. "Yahweh in the Hebrew myth, like Jocasta in the Greek myth, represents the infantile pleasure in self-centered ignorance of reality." Hence the Fundamentalist's detestation of "worldly wisdom," his constant reference to modern knowledge as "science falsely so-called"—following Paul's glorification of ignorance, based upon the Edenic mythology. "It is clear that the traditional interpretation of the Fall myth represents the wishes of the aging elders, the jealous parents, and the envious priests, the forces of reaction, and the unconscious wishes in every human soul to escape from life and to sink back into an unlimited indulgence of self-interested passivity. These wishes have remained in control of the educational authorities just because they are for the most part unconscious of their existence. . . . The person who forms his ideal according to the reality principle sees in the Garden of Eden myth, not the fall of man, but his ascent, and the triumph of his adult love of truth and reality over the passive pleasure-lust of babyhood. To choose ignorant dependence is to choose the arrest or regression of psychic life: to choose knowledge and disobedience is to advance towards adult individuality and self-guidance. . . . If sexual activity and sublimated displacements of primitive impulses are the normal conditions of psychical adulthood, it is essential that those who are wise as serpents should also feel as harmless as doves in spreading their knowledge about human life. . . . Sexual curiosity is a natural impulse in childhood; and the children's need for sexual knowledge is limited only by their capacity for understanding, which is indicated by the form of their questions. Consequently the dangers of harmful enlightenment are removed when truthful answers are given to all the inquiries of the young about sexual impulses in themselves and in society."

CHRISTIAN DOCTRINES IN PRE-CHRISTIAN AMERICA

There is not a single basic dogma of current Fundamentalism—Catholic or Protestant—which did not exist in Mexico before the discovery of America by the Christians. This startling statement I shall undertake to prove briefly by the remnants of Mexican records left by the invading conquerors, who burnt or destroyed otherwise everything they could lay their hands on. But first let us consider what it is that the present-day Fundamentalists believe and want us to believe with them.

Reduced to the barest outline, Fundamentalist theory affirms:

(1) There was a garden of Eden, in which the first man,

(2) Adam, was created out of the dust of the ground by the Creator of heaven and earth; and that the first

(3) Woman was fashioned by God out of a bone (rib) of the first man; that

(4) The first happy pair of innocent human beings was destroyed by a fallen angel—"the Devil"—in the form of a serpent, and was consequently expelled from the Garden of Eden, later becoming the ancestors of a race of sinful, inherently depraved, human beings.

(5) The Creator having realized his mistake, repented him, and mankind was destroyed by a universal deluge, a few human beings only being preserved from destruction by the

(6) Building of an Ark in which they es-

caped the flood, and which finally came to rest on the summit of an unnamed high mountain.

(7) Though continuing in "sin" (depravity) and "enmity to God," the human race was at last redeemed by a virgin-born Savior-God, of Nazareth, Palestine, who was condemned as an enemy of the Roman state and was crucified; thereupon he descended into hell for a period of three days and nights, when he arose from the dead, returned to his disciples in the flesh, and then ascended into heaven, whence he had come as the Son of the Creator, and whence he promised to return shortly "in glory."

(8) A Christian ecclesiastical organization was then developed, with a priesthood, churches, monasteries, convents, monks, nuns, rituals, the sacrament of baptism, the eucharist, holy water, crosses, altars, priestly vestments, etc.

Now, we have been taught that the events here mentioned, and the theology involved, the rites, ceremonies, symbols and so forth, are uniquely peculiar to what is regarded by our blatant Fundamentalists as "Christianity"—the one true religion, based upon "the word of God," "the revealed will of God," as found in the "Book of Books"; to wit, "the Holy Bible."

We may imagine the astonishment of the Roman Catholic priests who first landed in Mexico, under "the banner of Christ" and with the murderous Cortez, when they discovered that virtually all of the legends and institutions of "Holy Mother Church" were already known to the "heathen" whom they had come to instruct and "save"; that an almost complete replica of their own "only true religion" had already been established for years in Central America, centuries before the learned Fathers had been forced to concede that the earth is not flat, but round! that the devout Mexicans had already been "redeemed" by a crucified, virgin-born Son of God of their own!

In the legends and myths of the ancient Mexicans, we find stories and ideas which so closely parallel those of the Old Testament of the Hebrews that they suggest a common origin.

Like the Persians, Babylonians, and Hebrews, the ancient Mexicans had their myth of "war in heaven" and the "downfall of the rebellious angels." In the ancient Mexican, as in the Oriental myths, we are told of the first man's having been *made of clay*—a belief found also among the Cherokee Indians.

The first Mexican woman, like the Hebrew Eve, was fashioned *from a bone of the first man*. Furthermore, she is represented on the ancient Mexican monuments as apparently conversing with a huge male serpent. As in the case of Eve, the result of this amicable discourse was that she—as "spouse" of the Devil—became the mother of two sons (the result in Eve's case being, however, more indirect!). In the Mexican myth the boys were twins.*

---

*For further information on all these points see the following: Higgins, "Anacalypsis," Vol. II, p. 31; Squire, "The Serpent Symbol," pp. 67, 161; Wake and Westropp, "Ancient Symbol Worship," p. 41; Baring-Gould, "Legend of the Patriarchs and Prophets," p. 46; Doane, "Bible Myths," pp. 15, 533.

Like all the other peoples of antiquity *whose legends have come down to us*, the ancient Mexicans believed that man was born in sin, the human race being congenitally depraved, and deserving of condign punishment, even to the destruction of all but a few choice specimens of the race.

The Mexican "Noah," with six other *giants*—"There were giants in the earth in those days" (Gen. vi, 4)—built an ark in which they lived during a flood which destroyed all the Noahs of all the other races, along with their kith and kind and compatriots—the Mexicans being, of course, a "chosen people."

As in the case of the elect of Yahweh, of Palestine, the captain of the barge sent forth birds to search for a possible landing-place—the peak of some high mountain. In due time, an eminence was found, and the ark safely landed. The natives of various parts of Mexico and even of the contiguous territory, to this day show travelers the exact elevation on which the ark rested; just as in the Old World the Hebrews, Chaldeans, Armenians, Esthonians, Greeks, Hindus, Celts and others were able to point out—and some of them *still* point out—the exact peak on which *their* "Noah" landed.

(All these stories had, no doubt, a common origin; or, as a nature-myth, symbolizing the phenomena of winter, similar legends may, of course, have been developed by two or more people independently. In my own opinion, a common origin best explains the known facts.)

As in the Bible legend, the survivors of the

flood, or their descendants, determined that they should never again be caught the same way. So they resolved to build a mighty tower which should serve as a refuge in case of another cloud-burst, tidal wave, or similar catastrophe. And while they were about it, why not build a tower that should reach even to the windows of heaven—the abode of the gods? In Mexico such a lofty edifice was designed by Xelhua, surnamed "the Architect," one of the seven giants who were previously afloat in the ark; for Xelhua admitted that he was very curious to find out just what was going on in heaven. But the gods did not look with favor upon this daring project. So they, Jove-like, or Yahweh-like, hurled fire upon the rising pyramid, killing many of the workmen, and inflicted upon the survivors a "confusion of tongues." The builders then not being able to give or receive understandable orders, the effort to reach the very exclusive residential district of the immortals was abandoned. This tower (pyramid) was pointed out to both Alexander Humboldt and Lord Kingsborough on their famous visits to Mexico, and its ruins may still be seen at Cholula.*

The Mexicans also had their "Joshua" who caused the sun to stand still at his command.

But we must pass now to the "New Testa-

---

*See Kingsborough, "Mexican Antiquities" (or Higgins, Op. cit., Vol. I, p. 27); Brinton, "Myths of the New World," pp. 203-4; Squire, Op. cit. pp. 189-90; Humboldt, "American Researches," Vol. I, pp. 96-7. Cf. also Colenso, "The Pentateuch Examined," Vol. IV, p. 272.

ment" part of our Mexican story, with its "Roman Catholic" institutions—all in excellent running order before the Old World Christian system was ever heard of in America; or, it might well be, even before these doctrines were known in Europe or in Asia Minor.

Two thousand years, at least, before the Council of Ephesus (A. D. 431) declared that Mary, the mother of Jesus of Nazareth, was the veritable "Mother God"—the "Assumption" being declared in 813, and her Immaculate Conception in 1851 (by the Pope and Council)—the "pure virginity" of many other divine mothers had become an essential tenet of faith in the religious systems of the Old World. The Egyptian Isis, mother of the Savior Horus, was known as "Our Lady" and also as the "Queen of Heaven." She was adored many centuries before the origin of the Christian religion, and was represented with the infant Savior in her arms, just as were Maya, the virgin mother of Buddha, and Devaki, the virgin mother of Chrishna, in India. "Even in Mexico," says Dr. Inman ("Ancient Faiths," Vol. I, p. 100; see also p. 159), "the 'Mother and Child' were worshiped" as "Queen of Heaven."

The Mexican virgin mother was known both as Chilalman and as Sochiquetzal, and the infant Redeemed, or Savior-God incarnate, was known both as Quetzalcoatl and as Bacob. In the case of Mary of Nazareth, the annunciation was made through the agency of the Angel Gabriel. The Mexican representation of this solemn announcement to the virgin child that she was to become the mother of the Savior of her people shows an angel extending to her a bouquet of flowers.

Very suggestive is the fact that representations of the Virgin mother and infant Savior are often black. This is true in the case of the paintings and images of Isis and Horus, of Devaki and Chrishna, and in many cases of Mary and Jesus. The most ancient picture and statues in Italy and other parts of Europe, which are adored by the faithful as representations of the Virgin Mary and the infant Jesus, reveal the infant draped in white, but with the face black, and in the arms of a black mother. Images and paintings of this kind were seen by Mr. Godfrey Higgins, during the years 1825-35, at the Cathedral at Moulins, the famous Chapel of the Virgin at Loretto, the church of St. Stephen at Genoa, St. Francis at Pisa, St. Theodore at Munich, and elsewhere ("Anacalypsis," Vol. I, p. 138). The "Black Virgins" revered in certain French cathedrals "during the long night of the Middle Ages proved, when at last examined critically, [to be] basalt figures of Isis" (King, "Gnostics and Their Remains," p. 71; see also p. 109). The doctrine of the Mother of God is now thought to be of Egyptian origin. Dr. Inman tells us ("Ancient Faiths," Vol. II, p. 767) that "the head-dress, as put on the head of the Virgin Mary, is of Egyptian, Indian, and Grecian origin."

How does it "happen" that the Virgin Mother of the Mexican Savior-God so closely resembled the "Black Virgins" of Egypt and Europe? Had they not all a common origin?

Let us consider now the Mexican crucified Redeemer, Quetzalcoatl, or Bacob, "the son of God."

The symbol of this virgin-born Savior was, like that of a number of Eastern gods, the "Morning Star." His crucifixion is well represented in the paintings of the *Codex Borgianus* and in the *Codex Vaticanus*. Facsimiles of many of the paintings and hieroglyphics of ancient Mexico, which have been brought from that country and preserved in the libraries of Paris, Berlin, Dresden and Vienna, are reproduced in Lord Kingsborough's seven-volume work on the "Antiquities of Mexico" (London 1831).

In the Borgian MS. (p. 72), Quetzalcoatl is represented crucified upon a cross of Greek form, with nails through his hands and feet. His body, significantly enough, is covered with symbols of the sun (in other words, he is a Sun-God).

As in the story preserved in the Gospel According to Luke (xxiii, 44-45), at the time of the death of the Mexican Savior, "the sun was darkened and withheld its light" (Kingsborough). Like Jesus, Zoroaster, Osiris, Horus, Adonis, Hercules, and other virgin-born Redeemers, Quetzalcoatl "descended into hell" for a period of three days and nights. Like the Saviors just mentioned, and many others, including Baldur, the Scandinavian "Lord and Savior," the Mexican Christ "rose from the dead," and promised to return again in due time (cf. the "Second Advent" of orthodox Christians).

(The reason why the world's Savior-Gods were said to have been born on December 25th, and to have "descended into hell" for three days and nights following their "crucifixion," and then to have "risen from the dead," is well understood by comparative mythologists; but it is extraneous to the subject here.)

It is the tradition in Mexico that Quetzalcoatl assured the devoted inhabitants of Cholula that he would return again after his death to rule over them (Humboldt, Op. cit., Vol. I, p. 91), promising them great prosperity and happiness. "The Mexicans looked confidently to the return of their benevolent deity," says Prescott ("Conquest of Mexico," Vol. I, p. 60, Ed. 1873); just as the Jews awaited the coming of "the Messiah" who would restore their lost kingdom to more than its ancient glory; and just as the disciples of Bacchus (Dionysus) expected his second advent (Dupuis, "Origin of Religious Belief"). The Celts, Scandinavians, Teutons and Esthonians all had their Messiahs who were to return and restore them to happiness and wordly well-being.

An optimistic faith in the second coming of a Messiah, or Savior, has more than once led to baneful practical results. In the case of the Toltecs, the popular belief that "the Plumed Serpent" (as Quetzalcoatl was reverently called) would some day leave his place

GARDEN OF EDEN MYTH

among the gods and return in the flesh to lead his people, led to no evil consequences. But the same superstition, passed on to their successors, the Aztecs, caused a catastrophe. By one of those all but incredible coincidences which have from time to time completely changed the destiny of a nation, the adventurer and cutthroat Cortez landed in Mexico at the very time when, according to tradition, the "Plumed Serpent Savior" was to return. Even the spot at which the Spanish butcher of men landed was, according to a favorite legend, the very one from which the beloved Quetzalcoatl had launched his fabulous serpent-craft. With the approach of the huge "floating houses" of the Spanish conquistadors, with Cortez resplendent in shining armor, the rumor soon spread that the Plumed Serpent had returned. Even the great Montezuma fell a victim to the popular belief, and gladly welcomed Cortez as a veritable god. It was only a matter of a short time when the trusting people were slain and their wealth stolen, ending in the burning of the priceless literary treasures by the pious Roman Catholic vandal Diego la Landa and other agents of the Inquisition. "Of the fall of Mexico it was written in Aztec to the shame of Europe: *'Zan ye chocaya amaxtecatl'* (Then quickly wept the man of books)."

Of the grand masters of philosophy, of literature, of politics, who flourished before the Spanish sword introduced Christianity into America, there is hardly a syllable of understanding or praise. It was sad truth that the nameless Mexican bard put into words:

"For thy fame shall perish, Nopiltzan,
And thou, Tezozomoc, where are thy songs?"*

We hear much of the cruel human sacrifices of the ancient Mexicans. But Quetzalcoatl taught that "true sacrifice was personal and that the gods loved only the contrite heart."

Like Jesus and some of the other gods of the Old World, the Mexican Savior was "tempted" and "fasted forty days."

As among all the nations of antiquity, baptism by immersion or sprinkling, "for the remission of sins," was a common rite among the ancient Mexicans as well as among the Indians of South America—notably, the Incas of Peru. The Mexicans had a ceremonial baptism for infants which has been described by Prescott (*Op. cit.*, Vol. I, p. 64): "The lips and bosom of the infant were sprinkled with water, and the Lord was implored to permit the holy drops to wash away that sin that was given to it *before the foundation of the world*, so that the child might be born anew."

The Rev. Father Acosta, who wrote of the Indians of Mexico and Peru, alludes to this baptism by saying: "The Indians had an infinite number of other ceremonies and customs which resembled to the ancient laws of Moses, and some to those which the Moors use, and some approaching near to the Law of the Gospel, as the baths or *Opacuna*, as they called them; they

---

*Herbert J. Spinden, "What Is Civilization? The Answer of Ancient America," *The Forum,* September, 1925.

did wash themselves in water to cleanse themselves from sin" ("History of the Indies," Vol. II, p. 369).

After speaking of "confession which the Indians used," he says: "When the Inca had been confessed, he made a certain bath to cleanse himself, in a running river, saying these words: 'I have told my sins to the Sun [his god]; receive them, O thou River, and carry them to the Sea, where they may never appear more" (*Ibid.*, p. 361). He also tells us (p. 369) that the Mexicans had a baptism for infants, which they performed with great ceremony. "The ancient Peruvians also baptized their children" (Bonwick, "Egyptian Belief," p. 416). The Christian baptism, "in doctrine, as well as in outward ceremony, was precisely that of the heathen."

The Fundamentalist writers would have us believe that it was Jesus of Nazareth who *instituted* the sacrament of the breaking of bread and drinking of wine, supposed to be the body and blood of God. But the ancient Mexicans celebrated the sacrament of the Eucharist long before any European adventurers came to rob and enslave them—a sacrament which they called the "most holy supper." The bread—called *Tzoalia*—which they used at their Eucharist was made of corn meal, which they mixed with blood (instead of wine). This was consecrated by the priests, and given to the people, who ate it with humility and penitence, as the flesh of their god (Kingsborough, *Op. cit.*, Vol. VI, p. 220).

Acosta says that the Mexicans and Peruvians, in certain ceremonies, ate the flesh of their god, and called certain morsels of paste "the flesh and bones of Vitziliputzli" (*Op. cit.*, Vol. II, chaps. XIII and XIV).

"I am disposed," says the writer of the "Explanation of Plates of the *Codex Vaticanus*," "to believe that these poor people had the knowledge of our mode of communion, or of the communication of the gospel; or perhaps the Devil, being most envious of the honor of God, may have led them into this superstition [!], in order that by this ceremony he might be adored and served as Christ our Lord" (quoted in "Mexican Antiquities," Vol. VI, p. 221). As the pious Julius Fermicius, advisor to the emperors Constans and Constantius (318-365 A. D.), remarked, "the Devil has his Christs"; but the pagan priests, he joyfully observed, never administered the *genuine* Jesuine ointment.

It was probably the machinations of His Satanic Majesty which caused "the ancients" (so referred to by the Greek sophist Prodicus, in the fifth century B. C.) to worship bread as Demeter (Ceres) and wine as Dionysus (Bacchus). This sacrament was observed every fifth year at Eleusis, a town of Attica, in honor of Demeter, the goddess of corn, who, they said, had "given us her flesh to eat," as Bacchus, the god of wine, in a like allegorical sense, had "given us his blood to drink." Yet the unknown author of the Fourth Gospel (John, vi, 55), would have us believe that "these holy mysteries"—words derived from the Pagan ceremony of Eleusis (the Advent, or coming, from the common root)—are due to Jesus of Nazareth—"he that should come" (John, xi, 3).

One regrets to have to reflect that thousands of human beings have been savagely slaughtered on acconnt of differences of opinion concerning the Christian Eucharist. But among the Mexicans, of course, the whole "mystery" was the work of the Devil.

"Whoso shall merely look into it, shall find this manner which the Devil hath used to deceive the Indians, to be the same wherewith he hath deceived the Greeks and Romans, and other ancient Gentiles."*

The good Father Acosta was very much perturbed to find in Mexico, within the circuit of one of the beautiful temples, two monasteries, one for virgins, the other for men. Despite their worship of a "false Christ," the men were admittedly "profoundly devout," and "lived poorly and chastely," piously performing "the office of Levites" (*Op. cit.*, Vol. II, p. 336). Moreover, as witnessing their sincerity, "these priests and religious men used great fastings, of five or ten days together, before any of the great feasts, and they were unto them as our four ember weeks; they were so strict in continence that some of them [not to fall into any sensuality] slit their members in the midst, and did a thousand things to make themselves unable, lest they should offend their gods" (*Ibid.*, p. 339).

"There is one thing worthy of special regard,"

---

*Acosta, Rev. Joseph de, "The Natural and Moral History of the Indies," Vol. II, pp. 303-305. Translated by Edward Grimston, London, 1604.

Father Acosta further comments, "the which is, how the Devil, by his pride, hath opposed himself to God; and that which God, by his wisdom, hath decreed for his honor and service, and for the good and health of man, the Devil strives to imitate and pervert, to be honored, and to cause men to be damned: for as we see the great God hath Sacrifices, Priests, Sacraments, Religious Prophets, and Ministers, dedicated to his divine service and holy ceremonies, so likewise the Devil hath his Sacrifices, Priests, his kinds of Sacraments, his Ministers appointed, his secluded and feigned holiness, with a thousand sorts of false prophets" (Vol. II, p. 324).

Again: "We find among all the nations of the world, men expressly dedicated to the service of the true God, or to the false, which serve in sacrifices, and declare unto the people what their gods command them. There was in Mexico a strange curiosity on this point. And the Devil, counterfeiting the use of the church of God, hath placed in the order of his Priests, some greater or superiors, and some less, the one as Acolites, the other as Levites, and that which hath made most to wonder was, that the Devil would usurp to himself the service of God; yea, and use the same name: for the Mexicans in their ancient tongue call their high priests *Papes*, as they should say sovereign bishop, as it appears now by their histories" (Vol. II, p. 330).

Kingsborough quotes one Frances Hernandes, who wrote in 1545: "The Indians believed in the God who was in heaven; that this God was the Father, Son, and Holy Ghost, and that the Father was named Yzona, the Son Bacab [or Bacob], who was born of a Virgin, and that the Holy Ghost was named Echiah." Acosta also alludes to the fact that the Devil "after his manner hath brought a Trinity into idolatry" in Mexico; and tells of an image which the Mexicans called Tangatanga, "which they said was 'One in Three, and Three in One.'"

Having shown that the essential doctrines of Fundamentalism were—to all intents and purposes—in full bloom in the New World before any European ever set foot in Mexico (at least since the beginning of the Christian era), it remains now but to conclude with a few words relative to the circumstance that the Mexican Christ Quetzalcoatl was called "the Serpent God." There is nothing surprising about this; for the serpent has been connected with the Savior-Gods, and the demigods and legendary heroes, of all nations of antiquity.

Among certain early Christians, the "Ophites," the serpent was an emblem of Jesus himself. "As Moses lifted up the serpent in the wilderness, so must the Son of Man be lifted up."

"The Gnostics," says Irenaeus, "represented the Mind (the Son, the Wisdom) in the form of a serpent"; and "the Ophites," says Epiphanius, "have a veneration for the serpent; they esteem him the same as Christ." "They even quote the Gospels," says Tertullian, "to prove that Christ was an imitation of the serpent" (see Ferguson, "Tree and Serpent Worship," p. 9). Manes, in the third century, taught serpent worship in Asia Minor, under the name of Christianity, promulgating that Christ was an incarnation of the Great Serpent, who glided over the cradle of the Virgin Mary, when she was asleep, at the age of a year and a half" (see Squire, "Serpent Symbol," p. 246).

Apollo and Aesculapius were both originally worshiped under the form of a serpent; and the Phoenicians, Hindus, Egyptians, and other eastern nations venerated this animal: "The third member of the Chaldean triad, Hea or Hoa, was represented by a serpent. According to Sir Henry Rawlinson, the most important titles of this deity refer 'to his functions as the source of all knowledge and science.' Not only is he 'The Intelligent Fish,' but his name may be read as signifying both 'Life' and a 'Serpent,' and he may be considered as 'figured by the great serpent which occupies so conspicuous a place among symbols of the gods on the black stones recording Babylonian benefactors'" (Wake, "Phallism," p. 30).

That the ancient Pagan creeds, legends and myths—part of the universal *mythos*—should be found embodied in the religion of the ancient Mexicans, and that all these again are found to be but the original sources of the modern orthodox Christian religion, is by no means inexplicable, and need not be attributed to the subtlety of the Ubiquitous Devil. The explanation is that all religions and all languages of the civilized races of men had a common origin in an older seat of civilization.

Where that original center of culture was is another story.

DEBATING THE FUNDAMENTALISTS

George Bernard Shaw has recently diagnosed the anti-evolution crusade of our Fundamentalists as an exhibition of "infantilism." This is but one way of saying that Fundamentalism is an expression of "arrested development" of the cerebral cortex, a structure commonly referred to as "gray matter." The leaders of this aberrant group of morons—I use this term in a strictly scientific sense—are not distinguishable in physical appearance from normal individuals excepting—in many cases—by an orang-like close approach of the eyes to each other, leaving scarcely sufficient room between the visual organs for a very narrow nasal-bridge.

The speech-centers of the typical Fundamentalist brain seem to be rather highly developed, endowing them with a capacity for rapid discharge of words, though the vocabulary employed is by no means extensive, and the words used often have no rational bearing on the question supposed to be under discussion.

That the Fundamentalist opponent of evolution has absolutely no conception of the scientific principles involved in evolutionary theory becomes quite apparent to an intelligent listener after only a few minutes of his atavistic oratory.

Along with this native incapacity for comprehending the foundation principles of historical geology, of comparative anatomy, embryology, geographical distribution, the data of anthropology, etc., goes a certain shrewd disingenuousness, not to say intellectual dishonesty, which the Fundamentalist exhorter uses on his over-receptive victims with telling effect. (Debates with Fundamentalists mean debates before audiences of ingrown Genesiac persuasion, about 80 per cent of those present on such occasions being religiously and "unalterably" opposed to evolution before, during, and after the debate. With such "representative" audiences the Rileys "win" their debates, on a show of hands, or "a rising vote." *C'est a rire!*)

Needless to say, no scientific presentation of the evidences of evolution can be successfully presented for the benefit of an audience made up of men and women even farther below the level of rationality than their voluble spokesmen.

The proponent of evolution who innocently goes before a Fundamentalist audience with the expectation of convincing them by citation of irrefutable facts that plants and animals have come to be what they are now found to be by a gradual process of orderly development, or evolution, is courting not only a keen disappointment, but a veritable shock.

Facts to a Fundamentalist are either nonexistent or a device of the Devil. What interests and concerns him or her is "the Book," faith, miracles, original sin, redemption, etc., etc., and all else is but "the worship of reason," and a depraved lust for "science falsely so-called."

The Fundamentalist idea of evolution, or of

transformation of species, is that, if the doctrine of evolution is true, one genus, or even Order, of plants or animals should evolve from another "while you wait"—almost literally. Knowing this to be their conception of "Darwinism," in his first debate before a Fundamentalist audience the writer naively proceeded to explain that evolutionary processes, excepting for minor transformations or saltations, involved geological time and secular changes, sometimes even geological revolutions.

For example, it was pointed out that the developing groups of animals or plants should succeed one another in such a way that *the basic anatomical structures of the next higher group should be found already existing in the next lower.* The geological record was then utilized in proof of this claim. During the course of this systematic exposition of fundamental principles, it was shown how Birds were at first, and for many ages, but highly modified Reptiles.

"'But,' you quite naturally reply, 'Birds are feathered creatures, while Reptiles have no feathers.' Quite so. But it is now well established that feathers are but modifications of reptilian scales, both being merely developments of the outer or horny layer of skin. As one morphologist puts it, 'feathers are really scales with the edges of the scales frayed out.' Here, again, is illustrated the fundamental evolutionary principle that nothing comes by magical incantation, every organ or structure now existing in any higher class of animals being but a modification of some pre-existing structure. In no case do we get something from nothing."

Such a clear, simple statement of one of the undisputed results of modern research would be accepted as an established datum of evolutionary theory by an audience of normally developed human beings. But how was it greeted by a Fundamentalist audience? *By an uproar of derisive laughter!* But when reference was humorously made by the speaker to "that eminent scientist, Col. William Jennings Bryan," serious and prolonged applause followed.

Now what sort of "argument *against* evolution" does the Fundamentalist relish?

Here's a sample from a debate with the Rev. Dr. W. B. Riley, founder of "The World Christian Fundamentals Association," who admits that Luther Burbank and David Starr Jordan are his "equals" in the realm of science, but, alas! they need to come to Riley for correct conclusions on the question of evolution.

Said Riley (in the Los Angeles debate with the present writer): "I lived all of my boyhood on a farm, have raised lots of stock, but in all the years of my life I have never seen a sow give birth to a pup." (Loud and exultant applause from 4,000 Fundamentalists.) Thus was the evolutionary theory of the origin of species overthrown, the debate "won" by Dr. W. B. Riley, and Shipley backed off the platform, staggering under a humiliating defeat. The sow won!

Milton Keynes UK
Ingram Content Group UK Ltd.
UKHW020021061124
450708UK00001B/271